THRIVE AS AN EMPATH

HOW TO PROTECT AGAINST PSYCHIC VAMPIRES AND LEVERAGE YOUR SPECIAL GIFTS

BY SMART READS

Free Audiobook

ABOUT SMARTREADS

Choose Smart Reads and get smart every time. Smart Reads sorts through all the best content and condenses the most helpful information into easily digestible chunks.

We design our books to be short, easy to read and highly informative. Leaving you with maximum understanding in the least amount of time.

Smart Reads aims to accelerate the spread of quality information so we've taken the copyright off everything we publish and donate our material directly to the public domain. You can read our uncopyright below.

We believe in paying it forward and donate 5% of our net sales to Pencils of Promise to build schools, train teachers and support child education.

To limit our footprint and restore forests around the globe we are planting a tree for every 10 hardcover books we sell.

Thanks for choosing Smart Reads and helping us help the planet.

Sincerely,

Travis & the Smart Reads Team

TABLE OF CONTENTS

CHAPTER 1: ARE YOU AN EMPATH?

They say if you understand yourself really well, the world will be an easier place to live in. According to some people, emotional intelligence (which is the same as empathy) is more useful to us than an insanely high IQ. Having it means we connect better with people, and forge stronger, lasting relationships.

But what is an empath exactly? When you are affected by the energy of other people, you are an empath. When you intuitively perceive and feel what other people are feeling, you are an empath. In other words, you are in touch with other people's feelings just as much as your own. In this way, you have strong people skills, and are able to deal with different people from different backgrounds. Already, we can see why emotional intelligence is more useful than a high IQ, especially in the work place.

But there is much more to an empath than being able to connect with the feelings of other people. Aside from the positive aspects, such as being able to connect with others and understanding oneself better, there are parts of being an empath that can frustrate and wear you down. For example, it isn't always easy for an empath to distinguish between their feelings and someone else's.

But it's okay. Lots of people in this world are hugely empathetic, and they manage to work through the challenges their personality type presents. Moreover, once an empath is aware of their strengths and weaknesses, they are able to harness the former while forgoing the latter.

Let's take a look at a few of the common traits of an empath to find out if you have this personality type:

You Get Easily Bored And/Or Distracted
It takes a lot to hold an empath's attention. If work, home or even school life isn't offering enough intellectual and emotional stimulation, an empath will quickly grow bored and seek an alternative.

It can also affect social life, too. An empath craves stimulating and challenging conversations. If their friend isn't able to offer either, they will switch off and find other forms of entertainment. Perhaps they will doodle on a piece of paper or fiddle with their phones.

You Can't Do Things You Don't Actually Enjoy
To be compelled to actively do something, an empath must first know they are going to enjoy it. If an empath knows they won't enjoy something, they will refuse to do it. In the eyes of their friends, this could make them seem lazy or even stubborn. But an empath doesn't see the point in wasting their time doing something they know they won't enjoy.

Think about your life. Have there been times when an old friend has asked you to do a few things with them, only for you to turn them down? You like their company, but if the proposed activity is not to your liking, you see little to no point in engaging in it.

You Find It Difficult To Be In Busy Places

Because an empath responds strongly to the emotions and feelings of others, they often find it difficult to be in crowded places. Faced with such an overwhelming amount of people with various emotions and feelings, the empath can think only of an exit strategy.

Have you been in crowded places, such as sports arenas, malls and nightclubs, and felt uncomfortable? It could be you're finding it difficult to cope with all the emotions flooding into your system from other people.

You Just "Know" Things

This one is a little hard to describe because the sense of "knowing" an empath has goes beyond intuition. Basically, an empath just knows. They don't need to be told or explained something - they already know it. Most empaths would describe this sophisticated form of intuitive knowledge as exactly that - intuition or a gut feeling. But it's more than that. And the more the empath becomes aware of it, the more they tune into it. Subsequently, the stronger this "gift" becomes.

You Find It Really Hard To Watch Violence On TV

Because an empath is so in tune with the feelings of others, they find it almost unbearable to watch violence on TV. It is not that an empath is scared of violence in the same way a small child is. Rather, the empath is directly experiencing all the hurt and anguish of the character(s).

In a similar way, an empath can find it hard to watch the news or even read the newspaper. Eventually, they may break contact from all forms of media altogether as they seek to escape from a tumultuous wave of emotions that negatively affect their own state of mind.

You Root For The Underdog

An empath doesn't chase glory. Instead of always siding with winners, such as the world's top sports team, an empath instead roots for the underdog - the little guy who no one really expects to win. This is largely because an empath is drawn to those who are disadvantaged. It's the same when someone is faced with overwhelming odds that are stacked against them. An empath will always root in their favor.

Strangers Open Up To You

Even the empath themselves cannot explain this, but an empath has such an agreeable and open personality that strangers instantly realize this is a person they can be frank with. As such, a stranger will have no problems burdening the empath with their issues. Over time, the empath effectively becomes a sort of dumping ground for other peoples' woes. Eventually, these woes could become the empaths.

You Feel Tired A Lot

It's common for an empath to feel constantly tired because energy leeches are frequently draining them with their problems. Like leeches, these energy leeches attach themselves to the empath and burden them with their issues. Over time, these issues become a huge part of the empaths life. Eventually, they become saddled with so many problems they constantly feel worn out.

You Have An Addictive Personality
Empaths easily get addicted to things, be it substances, people, activities or even emotions. This can have a negative impact on their enjoyment of things. Because they commit themselves 100% to something, they react badly when it is no longer available. This is especially true in relationships or in situations of unrequited love (which can happen a lot for an empath). When an empath likes someone, they really like them.

You Like To Be Left Alone
Everyone likes alone time. As much as we are social animals, we all need our own space. But empaths need to be alone much more often than regular people. If they don't get enough time to themselves, they can start becoming uncomfortable. We can see early signs of empathetic behavior in young children who prefer to be left to their own devices. That isn't to say they can't or won't interact with other kids - they can and do - but they would prefer to spend a good amount of their time by themselves.

Why is this? There are many reasons, but one is that empaths respond heavily to the emotions of others. They become more physically and mentally drained than non-empaths. As such, they need time to refuel. Moreover, since they are always searching to uncover truths about themselves as much as other people, they need alone time to be able to do this.

You Are Interested In The Metaphysical
As well as metaphysical philosophy, empaths are also interested in alternative healing methods and holistic treatments. A number of empaths, indeed, will enter the field of medicine. However, this is not an easy field for an empath to enter, as it doesn't allow them to soak up other peoples' emotions. An empath who isn't aware they are an empath might enter the field of medicine, only to soon realize they made a mistake.

Empaths also like to read and learn about the metaphysical, or indeed anything otherworldly, such as the supernatural or the occult. They are not disturbed by stories non-empaths would probably find crazy, largely because they know we are prohibited by our five senses from truly being aware of the infinite possibilities that may actually exist.

An empath may also be a deeply spiritual person who finds it hard to explain their beliefs and reasons for their beliefs to non-empaths.

You Know When Someone Is Being Untruthful
According to Sicilian tradition, people have several "pantomimes" that give away the fact they are telling lies. But it's only an experienced Sicilian who is able to spot these pantomimes, and thus be in a position to call out a liar. However, empaths are also very good at detecting an untruth from a friend or family member This is largely because they understand human

emotions and responses better than the average person. They know the signs and they know what to look for. An empath is also able to detect when someone is being untruthful about how they feel.

You Are A Creative Person

Empaths tend to be creative people. Indeed, art itself is a very solitary vocation, and some of the world's most renowned artists spent large parts of their lives by themselves - which is a trait of an empath. Empaths might not stick to one artistic discipline, but may try their hand at a few, including dancing, writing, acting, singing, painting and so on. This is because an empath has a very rich imagination. Always coming up with new ideas, they need ways to express themselves and their thoughts. It's very possible some of your favorite writers, artists, singers, filmmakers and so on were empaths. Many creative people are.

You Value Animals

Everyone values animals. You would find it very hard to meet a person who claims to have not a single shred of care for any animal whatsoever! But empaths have a deep connection with animals, and many of them are vegetarians who refuse to eat animals that were slaughtered unnecessarily. But empaths don't merely refrain from eating animals - they will also spend a lot of their time with them. As such, there is a good chance that, if you are an empath, you have a few pets of your own at home.

Empaths care for animals in a way that they find it hard to turn away stray cats that visit often for food and milk. Eventually, there is a good chance the empath will eventually "adopt" the stray cat against their better judgment.

You Can't Fake Interest

Empaths get very bored easily in situations that don't stimulate them. But where non-empaths might find it easy to fake interest, empaths do not - even though they know it would probably be polite to do so. It's hard to get an empath to do something they don't want to, such as going to a sports game with a friend despite having no interest in sports whatsoever. But if you somehow manage to convince the empath to go along with the activity, it becomes near impossible for the empath to enjoy it or even fake enjoyment.

As such, the empath will usually just try to avoid such situations in the future, though doing so often sees them labeled disinterested, lazy or even boring and unadventurous by their friends.

Empaths And Paranormal Life Experiences

It is said empaths have supernatural experiences fairly frequently. Indeed, such experiences are common, and an empath may have a paranormal experience a number of times throughout their life. These experiences vary in their levels of intensity, but when they are super intense they can cause an empath to know themselves a whole lot more than they previously did. This period of "awakening" leads one on a path to inner knowledge and self-discovery.

Such experiences verge on the sublime can even be so intense and extreme as to be totally life affirming and life-changing. This is largely because such an experience is intended to make us more aware of who we are. The individuals who are unsure they are even empaths continue to live their life as a non-empath, undertaking menial chores and activities which aren't inspiring them. For an empathetic personality type, chores and tasks are so unrewarding and unfulfilling that they lack any kind of meaning or value. For this reason, it's crucial that an empath places themselves on a path that will inspire them to greatness.

Why You Need To Find You Path And Calling
A normal life and career is not really something an empath should settle for. The average man or woman might be inclined to settle down with a family, a mortgage, and a solid career, and indeed for most people this is their dream. But empaths are more imaginative and want more out of life. Not only do they not want to settle into a humdrum 9-5 way of life, but they physically or mentally can't. They have a very strong desire to carve out their own destiny and control every aspect of their life - especially their career.

Once you realize you're an empath, it's critical that you then listen to your true calling and follow it. Watch out for the signals. Listen to them and take heed. It's difficult because an empath often lives in a world surrounded by non-empaths who have already settled into a 9-5 lifestyle. As such, it's expected they will follow suit. But it's important to listen to your calling and be brave enough to do what feels right to you. If deep down you know you cannot live like those around you, make a stand for what you believe in. It takes courage, but it's important to make the first move. Otherwise, a life of misery and pain awaits.

The Curse That Was Meant To Be A Gift

Listen, empathy is a gift. The problem is it doesn't always feel like a gift. Indeed, empathy can create pain, hurt and even prolonged internal agony until we learn why we react in certain "programmed" ways to certain situations and stimuli. But it is a gift because it allows us to learn more about ourselves and those around us. You get an incredible chance to expand your awareness and this is a beautiful thing.

Crucial to being okay with this personality type is that we surround ourselves with people who understand and respect our unique gifts. The last thing we want is to hang out with those who seek only to exploit our unusually caring tendencies.

It is harder for a young person to come to terms with their empathic personality than it is an older person. But as the young person grows and matures, they develop a more sophisticated understanding and appreciation of self-respect and self-love. Over time, they become comfortable with the fact they are unique individuals who care for others, and who want to help as many people as they can. Compassion, after all, is a virtue.

CHAPTER 2: CHALLENGES OF BEING AN EMPATH

As outlined at the start of this book, there are two sides of the coin when it comes to being an empath. There are positive traits an empathetic personality has, which remind us that being an empath is a gift. But an empath also faces many daily challenges. Let's take a look at some of these:

Empaths Face Being Overwhelmed By External Stimuli

For empaths, feeling what is inside them is not always their biggest problem - instead, it is receiving external stimuli. We all exist in a world that is emotionally and karmically charged and empaths are more prone to receiving others people's emotions and karma more than anyone else. As a result, each day can be an overly intense - if rewarding - experience. For a non-empath, walking through rowdy crowds is easy. An empath, however, may want to avoid this - but they will find it hard to explain why to their friends.

In the event, an empath misses out on things their friends are attending and enjoying. Their friends - who don't understand why the empath is not joining them - will grow frustrated by their buddy's lack of interest or "sense of adventure." Empaths also get bothered whenever 2 types of music are playing at the same time. Again, this is not something that bothers non-empaths, but the empath will do what they can to avoid such a situation, as it can be deeply troubling.

Empaths Set Conflicts, Which Trip Them Up

Tuning into the energy of other people can exhaust an empath so much they have no time to even think about their own needs and feelings. An empath is usually friendly, approachable and open. They are not violent, aggressive or confrontational. If they witness conflict, they will play the role of peacekeeper - even though others are not always so appreciative of such a trait.

Emotionally charged situations are difficult to deal with for an empath. Whenever they come across an argument or any kind of conflict between two or more people, the empath will try and calm things down as quickly and as painlessly as possible. Either that, or they will just walk away. However, non-empaths (of which there are more than there are empaths) will often disregard the empaths attempts at instigating peace and reconciliation. Such a reaction can hurt the empath, who may then scurry back into their own private sanctum.

Empaths Defend Themselves - And Then Have To Live With The Regret

If an empath were to harshly scold someone during an argument while protecting themselves from verbal attacks, they will later look back with regret at their outburst. An empath always prefers to peacefully resolve issues as fast as possible. They regret it when they are roped into an argument, and especially regret it when they contribute to the prolongation of a conflict.

Many people are at odds with empaths because it is more common for an individual to gravitate towards conflict and exacerbate it. As such, non-empaths don't give a second thought to employing biting words, whether in the heat of the moment or not. An empath, on the other hand, finds life itself so intense that it is not so easy for them to handle.

Empaths Do Not Always Understand Their Personality

As humans, we switch through different moods as the day goes on. Perhaps we will start the day happy before something makes us miserable or even angry. The intensity at which someone experiences an emotion varies from person to person, but we all feel things. However, an empath feels much more than a non-empath. As well as being in touch with their own feelings, they are also in touch with the feelings of others. A veritable tsunami of emotions threatens to overwhelm and topple them, and can have a hugely negative impact on their day.

If a non-empath carelessly (and without realizing it) exposes their intense emotions to an empath before simply walking away, the effects on the former can be devastating. An empath wants and even needs a person to listen to them. It can make such a big difference to their mental wellbeing. Many empaths don't understand what is happening inside their hearts and minds; indeed, they are not aware anything special is going on at all. This is because they have yet to make the connection that their strong antennas have picked up other peoples' vibes and receptions.

Intense Mood Swings

When an empath is frequently absorbing other people's feelings and emotions, it's normal that confusion is going to reign. After all, it's difficult to explain why we feel great one moment and totally horrid the next. For this reason, an empath must work hard to understand themselves better. In this way, they will also discover what it is they can give to the world. Empathetic people have gifts that should be shared with others, but until they become aware of their gifts, they are of little to no use to anyone - including themselves.

Suppression

Empathetic people - like everyone else - develop defense mechanisms that help them cope with the world without resorting to conflict. Suppressing their true feelings is one tried and tested defense mechanism that always seems to work. Suppression of feelings may be born out of a bad childhood experience, or it may be a result of something that happened a bit later in life. Perhaps, for example, the empath was a shy teenager who learned it was more beneficial to them if they kept their feelings to themselves.

However, keeping their emotions locked up inside can have a negative effect on an empaths emotional wellbeing. Emotions, when suppressed, get stronger and stronger. Eventually, the empath will begin to feel overwhelmed and may experience neurosis, or even drug addiction as a way of dealing with their intense feelings. Physical ailments can even arise as a result of prolonged suppression.

Empaths Find It Hard To Watch Violent Movies
It's certainly not uncommon for a person to avoid violent movies or television shows. Such gory subject matter can make a person feel uneasy, and can play with their minds. But empaths have a much stronger aversion to on-screen violence than any other personality type.

Watching violence in a film or TV show can elicit powerful emotion responses in an empathetic person. They might cry, or they may even become physically ill - such as vomiting. An empathetic person will ask why a character could be so cruel, but the response "it's just a movie" isn't good enough. An empath simply cannot justify why there has to be violence on-screen and what the motivations behind the actions were.

Supernatural And Mystical Experiences
It's common for an empath to have a supernatural experience. But it's not easy for them to find a person who understands their experience. Consequently, the empath may suppress the experience, as well as their obvious gift for connecting with another world.

Because they do not feel as though they are properly understood or even listened to, an empath might dismiss their gifts and instead adopt the casual, skeptical attitude of a non-empath. No longer believing - or at least no longer wanting to believe - the empath suppresses some quite wonderful talents.

Adopting the attitudes of non-empaths is another defense mechanism, but it is one, which an empath should try to avoid. After all, it is natural for an empath to explore their gift for connecting with the supernatural, and suppressing their curiosity will only leave them frustrated and irritable.

Extreme Mood Swings
A lot of what we have said so far may have cast an empath in a negative light. But the truth is that empathetic personalities are fantastic listeners who are enthusiastic about life. They like to go out, and they like to have fun. And people enjoy hanging around with them. They also know how to laugh.

The problem is that extreme changes in mood often occur, so that an empath slumps from happiness to sadness in just a few moments. It isn't easy for non-empaths to understand this sudden change, and as such the non-empath may criticize their friends, telling them to "get a hold of themselves."

But it is natural for an empath to experience extreme mood swings, especially when you consider how vulnerable they are to being influenced by the moods of those around them. Like a cold, they "catch" these feelings and experience them.

CHAPTER 3: STRENGTHS OF AN EMPATH

Empathetic people tend to be humble and modest about what they have achieved. They find it easy to be enthusiastic about other people's achievements, but when the spotlight is trained on them, they find it hard to accept their qualities. As well as eulogizing others' achievements, an empath is also an open and honest person. These are two qualities which people like. An empath is generally very good at opening up about their feelings with other people.

Empaths are also good storytellers, who are able to hold the attention of an audience with their words. They have strong imaginations that captivate others.

Peacekeepers
Empaths are good at sensing how another person is feeling, and they tend to absorb and mirror those feelings. No topic of conversation is off-limits, regardless of how much conflict it may create. Such a personality ensures the empath is able to understand other people on the kind of level that allows them to play the role of peacekeeper in a potentially explosive situation. Indeed, it is not uncommon for a person to admit an empath understands more about them than they do themselves. This is because an empathetic person has a remarkable sense of understanding, and is able to penetrate into the depths of an individual's psyche.

Caring & Giving People

Empathetic people are giving and caring by nature. They take special pleasure in looking after other people, listening to them and supporting them. As such, it isn't uncommon to find an empath taking up a career working with animals, or in the field of medicine. Empaths also like to volunteer regularly, and do it for the sake of helping others, and not for any sort of recognition or monetary gain.

Appreciative of Music

Empaths find a lot of enjoyment and solace in music, and often take it much more seriously than non-empaths. They won't restrict themselves to one or two genres, but will seek out a variety of music styles, from classical to heavy metal, techno to jazz. They are willing to delve deeper than the mainstream in a bid to uncover hidden gems, and will give anything a go.

One of the reasons for this is that the empaths state of mind is constantly changing. As such, they require music that fits a certain mood, which might be different from a mood they were experiencing yesterday. Empaths are also highly influenced by the seasons, and as such will warm towards certain kinds of music in certain seasons. For example, they might avoid techno during the colder months, as it's a type of music that is generally associated with the summer.

Body Language

Empaths tend to utilize nonverbal communication often. They are very expressive in this regard, and will combine body language with forms of verbal communication. As such, it certainly isn't uncommon for an empath to enter the field of performing arts, either as a dancer or an actor, or an all-round performer. This is because they enjoy situations, which allow them to express themselves with their body. They have a remarkable ability to express complex thoughts, ideas and feelings through the medium of dance, acting and performance.

People Like Empaths!
Although being labeled an empath might sound troubling at first (few people, after all, enjoy being labeled), the truth is that, rather than trying to avoid empaths, people move towards them. They like to be around them. This is because in general empathetic people are super likeable. They are warm, friendly, and open. They are also sociable, and have a variety of friends who come from all walks of life. And despite sections of their friends finding it hard to get along with each other, the empath is able to get along with everyone.

CHAPTER 4: ADVANTAGES OF LIVING LIFE AS EMPATH

There are a number of advantages to being an empath. In fact, there are more advantages than there are burdens. Let's take a look at a few of these:

Empaths Are Good At Solving Problems

An empath is by nature a deep thinker who doesn't take things at face value. Instead, they look beneath the surface. For this reason, they are good at solving problems. An empath will obsessively look for an answer to something, and generally won't stop looking before a resolution has been made. If you happen to work alongside an empath, you'll naturally see this as an advantage. While other people may give up and admit defeat before finding the answer, an empath will keep on going. Empaths also look at the emotional aspect of a problem, which many people usually don't spot.

Good Team Players - And Leaders

A leader needs to have a number of qualities, but one of the most important is the ability to connect with everyone and make them all feel wanted and valued. Moreover, a leader needs to make sure a group of people harmonizes, despite their differences. These are people skills that not everyone possesses. Certainly, the world's top managers and sports coaches have these skills. Otherwise known as emotional intelligence, people skills allow you to lead in such a way that everyone is working towards the same goal without internal disruptions and conflicts.

Empaths, however, also tend to be quite shy people. But once you can convince an empath to lead, the warmth, openness and honesty they bring to the role invigorates everyone and makes them want to be on the empaths side, fighting for collective glory. Empaths are also great at answering concerns, and helping to rectify individual problems that might be holding someone back.

Wide Social Groups
Empaths don't stick to a certain kind of person when it comes to making friends. Rather than having just one personality type they always hang out with, empaths branch out and make friends with many different personality types.

This is because empathetic people by nature find it easy to relate to anyone, no matter how different one person is from another. They can relate to the eternal optimist as much as they can to the eternal pessimist. As a result, they always surprise people regarding whom they hang out with. Their friends might number a metal head, a nihilist, a Buddhist, a vegetarian, and even someone more aggressive and someone more peaceful.

A wide and varied group of friends means the empath is able to develop a stronger, more mature and well-rounded perspective of the world. Rather than seeing everything through a very narrow prism with just one viewpoint, they are able to look at things from a number of different angles. Their friends will also challenge them, and open their eyes to ways of thinking and seeing that they hadn't previously considered. As such, their knowledge of the world will enlarge, and their life will be rich with ideas. They will become more open and tolerant of people who are able to understand what motivates different people and what drives them.

For example, we don't always understand a custom or a behavior that is new to us. It's alien, and maybe we dismiss or criticize it. But by hanging out with a person who practices that custom or exhibits that behavior, we are able to better understand the motivations behind the customs and behaviors. Choosing to hang out with a very specific type of person narrows your world. Instead of casting light on things you don't understand, it keeps you mired in ignorance.

Vivid, Unforgettable Dreams
We all know someone who says they never dream, or that at least they never remember their dreams. For an empath, this is hard to believe because an empathetic person dreams often. Moreover, their dreams are often charged with emotions and are very vivid. And they also don't struggle to recall them. Empaths are often conscious of dreaming, and will slip into a lucid dream easily. Because they can spot the metaphorical meaning behind things - especially in art - they are also able to interpret their dreams with accuracy. During the next day, an empath might come

across something, which triggers memories of a dream they had the night before, and will then be able to recall it with amazing clarity.

As such, an empath is more in touch with their subconscious than a non-empath. They recognize that, not only does the subconscious exist below the threshold of consciousness, but it also carries weight because it influences our decisions and actions. Recognizing it and interpreting it is important, and an empath is able to do both of these things. An empath is not an expert on dreams. But because they are so in touch with the dream world, people may come to them for advice on their own dreams.

Magnetic And Creative People
People love to witness great feats of creativity. It's why millions upon millions of people have stood under Michelangelo's ceiling at the Sistine Chapel. It's why we give out awards to our best musicians and filmmakers. Creativity is an insight into human potential. It shows us what great beauty mankind is capable of.

Empathetic people tend to be really creative, and many will practice art, whether in their spare time or as a full-time career. As such, those people who do not create art themselves but who are impressed by creativity will warm towards an artistic empath.

Subsequently, an artistic empath has an advantage over people who are not artistic. With many people willing to talk and hang out with them, the empath is in a position to almost "handpick" who they want to associate themselves with - as well as who they want to take as their lover. This is a fantastic strength to have, as many of us are envious of those who are gifted and popular. However, as we have already mentioned, empaths can also be shy people. In this event, it is not easy for them to deal with a lot of attention, and they may even resent it at first. But once they understand their personality type, they are in a position to harness their gifts and use them to their advantage. They will soon see that an empathetic personality type is much more of a blessing than a curse.

Having such a magnetic personality type means the empath is in a position of strength when it comes to exerting a positive influence. Surrounded by a lot of people, the empath is able to use their gifts for helping others. They can spread positive vibes, and remind people anyone can do anything if they put their minds to it and take the right action.

Forging Strong Bonds With People
People don't find it difficult at all to open up with an empath, and they are even willing to share secrets they have so far kept close to their chests. As such, empaths forge very deep and strong friendships with people. Empaths are trustworthy, and individuals have little problem welcoming them into their lives.

If you can captivate someone's imagination, you have his or her undivided attention. Empaths enjoy talking to people who have experienced life and have things to say, much more than they enjoy talking to people who have a lot of academic knowledge, but who don't really have any kind of life experience. They might be good at recycling Plato's thoughts, but, not having put anything into practice, their words don't have a lot of value or substance. They lack the kind of insight that comes from day to day experience.

Synchronicities
An empathetic person is in touch with things that are not seen, and this can cause things to happen that cannot be explained so easily by saying it was just a coincidence - such as deja vu, the feeling that one is replaying a moment that has already occurred at some other stage in their life. And the more the empath connects to their true self, the more often they will experience magical and strange moments.

Connecting To Other Dimensions
Just like an empath has a bigger connection with dreams that non-empaths don't have, they also have a connection with realms which most of us don't see. An explanation for this is the aura that wraps around them, becoming a part of them. The aura is at its strongest when the person is focusing on it and encouraging it. When they downplay it - or flat out deny its existence - the aura is naturally not so potent.

Being connected with other realms and dimensions means the empathetic personality has a peerless depth that gives them every opportunity to live life to its fullest, experience everything with amazing clarity and feeling. In conclusion to this chapter, it isn't hard to see that an empathetic personality has a lot to be excited about. The more they understand themselves, the stronger they will become.

An empath should not suppress their gifts or get down simply because they are different to those around them. Instead, they should run with this otherness and use their unique gifts to their advantage. After all, when a person has a gift they surely have a duty to use it. Would you be happy if you knew someone who had an ability to solve a problem, but opted not to use it because they were the only one who had the ability? You would be frustrated.

Unfortunately, it has become human nature to look for validation for our actions from other people. If we see other people acting in certain ways, we are likely to copy them.
If we see no one who shares our traits, we may suppress them. However, as an empath you have strengths and advantages that a lot of other people don't have. This puts you in a unique position. Use it wisely. Don't be afraid or embarrassed by your gifts, but harness them.

CHAPTER 5: HOW TO MAKE LIFE EASIER

Despite the advantages of being an empath, life can still be difficult and emotionally exhausting. The good news is there are ways to simplify life so that it is more manageable. Once you have simplified your life, you'll be able to shine. In chapter five, we will look at how to make life easier.

Identify What Your Boundaries Are
When you don't know what you can't and can handle, life can be really tricky as an empath. Only when you know what works for you and what doesn't are you able to harness what is healthy while discarding what is unhealthy. This might mean cutting someone from your life who is constantly bringing you down and making you feel negative. It might sound harsh, but what's important here is your own equilibrium.

The problem an empath has when it comes to setting boundaries is that they often find it hard to say "No" to someone. Essentially, you need to integrate your limits not into just your mind, but also into your body. Practicing yoga can help, as it lets you bring your focus into your core.

Regulate Intimacy
Intimacy for an empathetic personality type comes down to reciprocity and space. Sometimes, you crave intense physical, spiritual and emotional bonding, and sometimes you crave the opposite - you want your own personal space. You want people to leave you

alone. The problem is that an empath craves extremes, and it can be off putting to other people. When you want to hang around other people, you can alarm them with your need for contact. When you want space, you can appear antisocial and remote.

Moreover, because you're naturally a giving person, it can be hard to reciprocate. To strengthen your ability to receive attention from other people, you could try yoga or bodywork. But it must be with someone who you trust and care for. It's also recommended you practice yoga with other people, as it will solidify your sense of community.

Unravel Emotions

Empaths absorb the feelings of others. Consequently, they lose sight of their own feelings. This can be damaging as it causes you to lose a sense of self. Spending time alone allows you to understand yourself more. You are able to distinguish someone else's emotion from your own. This is not something you are able to do when people constantly surround you.

Focus On Your Creativity

A lot of empaths are creative people. Creativity is in fact a very common trait that many people with this personality type have. When they're feeling blue, or whenever the world just doesn't feel right to them, an empath may seek shelter by doing something creative. This could be anything, from a piece of art to poetry. Anything you can think of. It's important that as an empath you feed your creative soul. For an empath, creativity is as important as sunlight is to a plant. For happiness and emotional wellbeing, it is important that you satisfy the creative aspects of your personality.

CHAPTER 6: PROTECTING YOURSELF FROM ENERGY LEECHES

Because empaths quite literally "feel into" the feelings and emotions of other people, they can be left feeling overwhelmed and exhausted. Basically, an empath can have the life drained out of them by so-called energy leeches who are unwittingly flooding the empath with their emotions. The empath is vulnerable to something we can call emotional contagion.

But let's take a look at what an energy leech is exactly. An energy leech is a person who is generally negative. Common emotions for them are sadness, fear, anxiety and even anger, and hanging around them can consequently be a chore - especially for empaths.

Of course, non-empaths don't find it such a chore to hang around energy leeches. They are not as attuned to the emotions of other people, and perhaps they won't even be able to tell you if someone is overly negative. An empath, however, can.
By virtue of their compassionate nature, an empath will often feel as though it's their duty to help energy leeches who are struggling with strong feelings and overwhelming emotions. It doesn't matter whether the person is a family member, a friend or even a total stranger. The empath will always feel compelled to help out.

The problem is that an energy leech is the only person who can truly help themselves. An empath might try to help them, but they will ultimately fail. However, all the effort they put into helping the person is what leaves them exhausted and bereft of energy. The energy leech has "sucked" all their energy out of them.

Common Traits Of An Energy Leech:

Insecurity
Human beings are insecure by nature. Everyone is insecure about something, and we all have moments where we're unsure of ourselves. But energy leeches tend to be way more insecure than anyone else. They look for validation from their friends and even strangers, and constantly ask people questions such as "Am I intelligent?", "Do I look good in this?" and "Do you really like me or are you just saying that?"

As mentioned, everyone asks questions like this at some point or another. But an energy leech is someone who constantly repeats these questions and similar ones. And it doesn't matter how often or even how strongly you assure the energy leech that everything is fine and that they look great. They will never be satisfied with your answer, and will ask again the next day. The reason for this problem is unquestionably theirs, and only THEY can solve it. You might think you're doing them a favor by providing solutions, but the reality is you're just harming yourself. At the same time, you are not even improving their situation - despite your good intentions.

Anger

The last kind of person an empath needs to hang around is a volatile, angry person who is capable of flipping out at any moment. Although anger is just another emotion like any other, an empathetic person gets distressed when anger is expressed in their company. They absorb this powerful emotion, and it has the potential to knock them out of their stride for the next few hours.

So while a non-empath can recognize when anger is not being directed at them but is just a general outburst of frustration on the part of the person who is expressing the emotion, an empath may take it personally - which can be really harmful.

Jealousy

As mentioned earlier, empaths are generally creative people who are possessed with a magnetic personality. As such, people are attracted to them; they want to hang out with empaths in order to get to know them better.

However, this puts the empath in a rather precarious position. People who are naturally inclined to feel jealous of others will notice how popular the empath is and they will make attempts to bring them down, usually as a result of their own insecurities. An empath is usually unaware when another person is jealous of them. As such, they will become disheartened as a result of the unjustifiably harsh way that they are treated.

Although we have said throughout this book that an empath is better at recognizing and responding to the emotions and feelings of other people than non-empaths, it is not so easy for them to spot jealousy. This is because an empath doesn't accept that they have qualities, which others admire - and are even jealous of. And if they do accept these qualities, it is a long time before they get to this point.

Questions You Need To Ask Regarding Energy Leeches

Is this person adding value to my life?

Ask yourself whether or not a person you suspect is an energy leech is adding any value to your life, or if they're just draining you of valuable energy. What do they do for you? Do they impact you positively by inspiring or encouraging you? Or do they just make you feel exhausted?

Try to recall five times you have met a person you suspect to be an energy leech, and write down the pros and cons of each meeting. Then, consider how the experiences shaped your mood, and how they left you feeling afterwards. Did you feel content or even happy? Or did you feel physically and mentally drained to a point where you felt morose and reflective?

I Spend Time With My Friend - But Is It Just Because I Feel Guilty?

Have you ever spent time with a friend and then thought, "Well, that was a total waste of time!" If spending time with a friend is a total waste of time, it's important that you start to question your reasons for hanging out with them. And you might find that the reason you're still hanging out with them is because, thanks to their problems and the fact that you two have been friends for sometime now, you feel guilty or even obligated.

This is not a good enough reason to hang out with someone and you should immediately stop if you cannot think of a better reason to see a friend. Proper friends are more than obligations.

If My Friend Wasn't Around, Would I Actually Feel Better About My Life?
We all have "friends" who actually make us feel worse than we should. They drain us with their negative outlook and their constant put-downs. Although they say they have our best interests at heart, this can't be true if all they do is leave us feeling bad about ourselves and life in general.

Try to picture what your life will be like if your friend is taken out of the frame. What can you see? Is it better, the same, or worse? Has a void been filled or opened up? If the answer is that, Yes, life is better, you seriously need to reevaluate your friendship and the amount of time you spend with that person.

Dealing With Energy Leeches You Can't Avoid
You can't always identify an energy leech before kicking them out of your life. What if your boss is one? Although that scenario is unlikely, you get what I mean. There will be energy leeches you have to work with closely. Here is how to deal with them:

Watch How They Effect You

To be able to guard yourself from other people's negative emotions, you need to pinpoint how the emotions are affecting you. Doing this allows you to distinguish your own feelings from those transmitted by others. Put simply, you will not be able to deal with external emotions until you learn how to identify them.

But how do you do this? You could start by writing down the various emotions you feel throughout the day. Then, at night, you could read through the list and recall any incidents that may have caused a shift in your emotions. Perhaps moments before you became flustered, Bob from HR was projecting something onto a colleague next to you.

Don't Own It

Empaths catch emotions like we all catch a cold, and it will take some time before they realize what happened. Once you notice your mood is changing, take a moment to consider why it is changing. Have you caught someone else's emotion, perhaps? If so, recognize this and then decide you are not going to own it. It is their emotion - not yours.

Don't Engage

The moment an empath starts to engage an energy leech is the moment disaster can strike. Once you allow yourself to get involved in drama, there is often no easy way out. Not only can this take up your time and leave you feeling exhausted, but it also dramatically alters your own mood and leave you feeling disappointed when you realize you haven't been able to help them. Engaging them doesn't make them feel any better. It just involves you in their feelings. For you and for them, there is really no value in getting overly involved in their affairs.

CONCLUSION

There has never been a more succinct saying than "know thyself." Once you understand yourself and what you can offer the world, you are in a much better position to double down on your strengths while either eliminating your weaknesses altogether or using them to your advantage.

So what's next? It's now up to you to harness your strengths. As an empath, you have amazing gifts to share with the world, which can brighten your life and the life of those around you. And perhaps more importantly - avoid the leeches!

THANKS FOR READING

We really hope you enjoyed this book. If you found this material helpful feel free to share it with friends. You can also help others find it by leaving a review where you purchased the book. Your feedback will help us continue to write books you love.

The Smart Reads library is growing by the day! Make sure and check out the other wonderful books in our catalog. We would love to hear which books are your favorites.

Visit:

www.smartreads.co/freebooks

to receive Smart Reads books for FREE

Check us out on Instagram:

www.instagram.com/smart_readers

@smart_readers

Don't forget your 2 FREE audiobooks.
Use this link www.audibletrial.com/Travis to claim
your 2 FREE Books.

SMART READS ORIGINS

Smart Reads was born out of the desire to find the best information fast without having to wade through the sheer volume of fluff available online. Smart Reads combs through massive amounts of knowledge compiles the best into quick to read books on a variety of subjects.

We consider ourselves Smart Readers, not dummies. We know reading is smart. We're self taught. We like to learn a TON about a WIDE variety of topics. We have developed a love for books and we find intelligence attractive.

We found that each new topic we tried to learn about started with the challenge of finding the pieces of the puzzle that mattered most. It becomes a treasure hunt rather than an education.

Smart Reads wants to find the best of the best information for you. To condense it into a package that you can consume in an hour or less. So you can read more books about more topics in less time.

OUR MISSION

Smart Reads aims to accelerate the availability of useful information and will publish a high quality book on every major topic on amazon.

Smart Reads hopes to remove barriers to sharing by taking the copyright off everything we publish and donating it to the public domain. We hope other publishers and authors will follow our example.

Our goal is to donate $1,000,000 or more by 2020 to build over 2,000 schools by giving 5% of our net profit to Pencils of Promise.

We want to restore forests around the globe by planting a tree for every 10 physical books we sell and hope to plant over 100,000 trees by 2020.

Doesn't it feel good knowing that by educating yourself you are helping the world be a better place? We think so too...

Thanks for helping us help the world. You Smart Reader you...

Travis and the Smart Reads Team

WHY I STARTED SMART READS

Every time I wanted to learn about something new I'd have to buy 20 books on the topic and spend way too long sorting through them and reading them all until I arrived at the big picture. Until I had enough perspectives to know who was just guessing, who was uninformed and who had stumbled upon something remarkable.

I wished someone else could just go in and figure that out for me and tell me what matters. That's how smart reads was born. I want smart reads to be a company that does all that research up front. Sorts through all the content that is available on each topic and pulls out the most up to date complete understanding, then have people smarter than me package the best wisdom in an easy to understand way in the least amount of words possible.

For example, I got a new puppy so I wanted to learn about dog training. I bought 14 different books about dog training and by the time I got through the first 5 and finally started getting the big picture on the best way to train my puppy she had grown up into a dog.

Yeah she's well behaved. She doesn't poop in the house. I can get her to sit and come when I call. But what if someone else went in and read all those books for me, found the underlying themes and picked out the best information that would give me the big picture and get me right to the point. And I'd only have to read one book instead of 15.

That would be amazing. I would save time. And maybe my dog would be rolling over, cleaning up after my kids and doing the dishes by now. That my friend, is the reason I started smart reads. Because I wanted a company I can trust to deliver me the best information in an easy to understand way that I can digest in under an hour. Because dog training is one of many subjects I want to master.

The quicker I can learn a wide variety of topics the sooner that information can begin playing a role in shaping my future. And none of us knows how long that future will be. So why not do everything we can to make the best of it and consume a ton of knowledge. And I figured all the better if I can also make a positive difference in the world.

That's why we're also building schools, planting trees and challenging ideas about copyright's place in today's world. Because as a company we have to be doing everything we can to support the ecosystem that gives us all these beautiful places to read our books. Thanks for reading.

Travis

Customers Who Bought This
Customers Who Bought This Book
Also Bought

Success Principles: Techniques for Positive Thinking, Self-Love and Developing a Powerful Mindset

Kundalini Awakening: Techniques To Raise Your Shakti Energy

Meditation for Beginners: Overcome anxiety, relieve stress, fight depression, conquer fear, find inner-peace, happiness, mindfulness

Develop Self-Discipline: Daily Habit to Make Self Confidence and Will Power Automatic

Dealing with Anxiety: Modern Techniques for an Age Old Condition

Self-Esteem Supercharger: Build Self Worth and Find Your Inner Confidence

Neuro Linguistic Programming: NLP Techniques for Hypnosis, Mind Control, Human Behavior, Relationship, Confidence

Meditation Magic: Free Yourself from Worry, Depression, Stress and Anxiety

www.ingramcontent.com/pod-product-compliance
Lightning Source LLC
Chambersburg PA
CBHW072121280526
45788CB00006B/2580